Modern Nutrition for Recreational Marath Runners:

Using Your Resting Metabolic Rate to Stimulate Muscle Growth, Add Energy to Your Training, and Outlast the Competition

By

Joseph Correa

Certified Sports Nutritionist

COPYRIGHT

ACKNOWLEDGEMENTS

The realization and success of this book could not have been possible without the motivation and support of my family.

Modern Nutrition for Recreational Marathon Runners:

Using Your Resting Metabolic Rate to Stimulate Muscle Growth, Add Energy to Your Training, and Outlast the Competition

By

Joseph Correa

Certified Sports Nutritionist

CONTENTS

Change your nutritional lifestyle now to get long term results and faster recovery times

CHAPTER 5: High Protein Calendar

Planning for success one day at a time

CHAPTER 6: High Protein Muscle Recipes

Easy to follow recipes to increase muscle

ABOUT THE AUTHOR

As a certified sports nutritionist and professional athlete, I traveled around the world and competed against some of the best. Being able to share what I have learned is important to me. My knowledge and experience has helped my students throughout the years. The more you know about what to feed your body, the better you will do.

If you want to see long term results in a healthy and realistic manner, than this book will do that for you.

Adding supplements or performance enhancers is a decision you have to make on your own. Always consider what side effects or long term changes your body will have before starting since that should be your primary concern. Finding organic and natural sources are always a better alternative.

INTRODUCTION

Modern Nutrition for Recreational Marathon Runners will show you how to add lean muscle mass in order to increase your RMR and accelerate your metabolism. If you want to make a serious change on your body and how it performs on a daily basis, you need to read this book and start applying it in your daily life.

What is RMR?

RMR is your resting metabolic rate. Your Resting Metabolic Rate measures the amount of energy used by your body in a resting or relaxed state.

How does RMR work?

RMR is the greatest component of energy expenditure in your body and so it tells us just how much energy and fat your body burns on a daily basis. By adding lean muscle mass you automatically increase your RMR which can lead to improved performance with long lasting results.

What benefits can I have from accelerating my resting metabolic rate?

Accelerating your RMR will lead to having more energy, adding more muscle, dropping unwanted fat, reduce injuries, improve your focus and concentration, etc.

Does this book have a calendar I can follow?

Yes, an easy to follow calendar is provided.

Will this book provide me with recipes I can use and prepare on my own?

Yes, simply and easy to prepare recipes are explained in detail so that you can get started right away.

Eating complex carbohydrates, protein, and natural fats in the right amount and percentages as well as increasing your RMR will have many positive effects such as making you faster, stronger, recover quicker, develop muscle at an accelerated rate, and become more resistant.

CHAPTER 1

Modern Nutrition for Recreational Marathon Runners

Using Your Resting Metabolic Rate to Stimulate Muscle Growth, Add Energy to Your Training, and Outlast the Competition

The key to getting in better shape is simply eating right and exercising. Doing those two things the right way is what this book is about.

Why are we focusing on the answer to your problems first?

Knowing what needs to be done does not guarantee that you'll know what steps need to be taken to get there!

There's always something in life that you end up neglecting and later regretting. This is specifically true with health. Usually, physical problems start small and then go on to become very difficult to manage and that's why we need to prevent them starting with our youth.

All athletes should eat a lot of fruit, vegetables, and protein derived foods (chicken, eggs, turkey, fish, etc.). Complex carbohydrates intake should be cut down to a maximum of brown rice, pasta, all natural bread, and organic ingredients.

In some places around the world where people have the longest life spans we can see several things in common: they drink mostly water, natural fruit juices, and milk. Everything they eat and drink is composed of natural, non-processed, non-canned, and non-preservative containing foods. By using this knowledge about people with longer life spans and their eating habits and other medical facts, I have created a nutrition guide that will help you to live and compete healthier and to live longer. It will also allow you to control your weight and the shape of your body better.

This book is divided into 3 marathon lifestyles:

Low Cardio Lifestyle Athlete (LCLA):

This dietary phase is for athletes who require less food containing complex carbohydrates (these include but are not limited to: pasta, brown rice, oatmeal, brown beans, lentils, etc.). These people do not need to store up that many energy reserves and therefore should have a higher percentage of foods containing proteins, legumes, vegetables, dairies fruits and other.

LCLA is for athletes who don't do more than 30 minutes of cardio per day as part of their training and also during competition. You can be flexible during competition since some conditions and environmental changes might change just how you can absorb food. This could be because of the country you are competing in, or you might feel nauseous before competing, or it can also be because of the food available in that area.

After the first month of completing this diet phase and complementing it in combination with your regular physical training regiment, you can decide to continue or adapt the diet to your needs in case you feel you need to add more protein or carbs or dairies.

Medium Cardio Lifestyle Athlete (MCLA):

This dietary phase is for athletes who require a specific percentage of foods containing complex carbohydrates (these include but are not limited to: pasta, brown rice, oatmeal, brown beans, lentils, etc.) to maintain a medium cardio-intensive lifestyle, while at the same time consuming a higher percentage of foods containing proteins, dairies, legumes, and fruits.

MCLA is for athletes who complete a minimum of 30 minutes of cardiovascular workouts as part of their daily physical training which may include (if you cross-train): swimming, walking, running, bicycling, jumping, rowing or playing sports that combine any of the aforementioned activities.

High Cardio Lifestyle Athlete (HCLA):

This dietary phase is for athletes who require a larger percentage of foods containing complex carbs to maintain their cardio intensive lifestyles in a balanced and healthy manner, while still maintaining a high percentage of foods containing protein, legumes, vegetables, fruits, and nuts.

HCLA is for people who train more than an hour of daily cardiovascular exercise. At least one hour of high intensity cardio workouts include (if you cross-train): running, swimming, rowing, jumping, or bicycling. This is especially important for athletes who do a lot of cardiovascular exercise as they require more carbohydrates to stay in good physical shape and to allow their bodies to recover.

The USDA Food guide pyramid contains the following groups of food:

a) Bread, Cereals, Rice, Pasta Group (6 to 11 servings): This group consists of the carbohydrate heavy foods and is placed at the bottom of the pyramid indicating that they should be eaten more often and should form an important part of the daily diet. The rationale behind eating more carbohydrates is that they provide energy so that a person is required to eat less fat. It is recommended that a person should have 6-11 servings from this group.

b) Vegetables (3-5 servings) and Fruit (2-4 servings): There is no doubt that fruit and vegetables are good for the body. Fruit and vegetables provide the body with essential vitamins and other nutrients and ward off diseases and ailments. A person should have 3-5 servings of vegetables and 2-4 servings of fruit a day.

c) Meat, Poultry, Fish, Dry Beans, Eggs and Nuts Group (2-3 servings): This group provides the body with proteins. Proteins help in building the body tissues and muscles. A person should eat 2-3 servings from this group a day.

d) Milk, Yogurt and Cheese Group (2-3 servings): This group provides proteins and calcium that make the bones strong and prevent health problems related to the degeneration of bone mass. A person should eat 2-3 servings from this group a day.

e) Fats, Oils and Sweets (eat sparingly): This group should be eaten sparingly. Fat leads to heart disease and obesity. Too much sugar also leads to obesity which can later create health problems in the future.

The food guide pyramid provides an excellent way to ensure that the body's nutritional requirements are fulfilled properly. By following the guide, an individual will receive all the daily requirements in terms of energy, proteins, vitamins and other essential nutrients.

Here are the recommended sizes of the servings for foods high in carbohydrates.

Vegetables: 1 cup of raw vegetables, or ½ a cup of cooked vegetables, or ¾s of a cup of vegetable juice.
Fruit: 1 medium sized fruit (such as 1 medium sized apple or 1 medium sized orange), ½ a cup of a canned or chopped fruit, or ¾s of a cup of fruit juice.
Bread and cereals: 1 slice of bread; 1 ounce or 2/3 s of a cup of ready-to-eat cereal; ½ a cup of cooked

rice, pasta, or cereal; ½ a cup of cooked dry beans, lentils, or dried peas. Dairy: 1 cup of skimmed or low fat milk.

The proper intake of proteins, fats and carbohydrates for non-athletes is:

Proteins 12%

Carbohydrates 58%

Fats 30%

The proper intake of proteins, fats and carbohydrates for athletes is:

Proteins 15-25%

Carbohydrates 50-65%

Fats 10-25%

Body builders eat more proteins to add muscle and bulk, with the proteins accounting for up to 35-40% of the diet for professional body builders.

Aerobic vs Anaerobic Physical Activity:

There are 2 main types of physical activity: Aerobic activity and anaerobic activity.

Anaerobic activity is defined as the activity undertaken without the presence of oxygen which cannot be sustained for long periods of time. This type of activity relies heavily on the fast twitch muscle fibers. Examples of anaerobic activity are weight lifting and sprinting. Such activities cannot be undertaken for long periods of time. This type of activity helps in building lean tissue and improves the body composition. The anaerobic capacity test is a test that measures the ability of the body to undertake exercise of a short duration and of a very high intensity. The Wingate cycle test is commonly used to test anaerobic capacity. Aerobic Fitness, also known as cardiovascular fitness is the ability of the body to perform an exercise over an extended period of time in the presence of oxygen. This type of activity relies heavily on slow twitch muscle fibers.

A training program which combines cardiovascular fitness and muscular fitness allows more oxygenated blood to be delivered per beat and increases the myoglobin in the muscles so that they can take up more amounts of oxygen, thus allowing more work to be done. This is why it is a smart decision to cross train. In marathons, being able to combine both aerobic with anaerobic training will give you the best results before, during, and after competition.

HELPFUL TIPS:

- Keep any condiments in your food to a minimum of one teaspoon per meal. Just enough to give your food some flavor.
- Instead of sugar, use honey to sweeten your drinks and food. If you absolutely have to use sugar make sure it's brown sugar.

Sports nutrition is more than just what you eat;

It's when and how you eat!

Drink at least 6-8 glasses of water per day

Drink 1 glass of water when you wake up, 1 before every meal, and 1 before going to sleep.

Eat 6 small to medium size meals per day

You should be eating every three hours. Use a timer, a stop watch or your cell phone to keep track of time as this is just as important as what you eat. If you eat small to medium size meals every three hours, you allow your body to digest food in an efficient manner and in a way that does not overwork the digestive system. Some people eat three large meals a day and then have to wait several hours until they don't feel full again but this is exactly what not to do.

Chew then swallow!

Sounds simple enough, but with today's busy schedules people tend to skip chewing and go directly to swallowing. That won't allow your body to process food the way it should, so make sure you take the time to chew your food. Your teeth have a purpose and that purpose is to break down food before it gets to your stomach so that it may do what it was intended to do. Remember, not chewing your food means your stomach has to work harder and that equates to a longer wait time for digestion that may cause you discomfort or gas.

No carbs or fruit after sunset

There's no need to store up energy you're not going to use while you sleep. Try to stay away from large meals after sunset. Be sure to consume a healthy snack if need be to prevent yourself from overeating during those times or simply drink a glass of water.

Always find time to exercise or do some form of stretching when you wake up, as this is the ideal time of day to get in shape and stay injury free.

Nutritional Guide for L C L A's

Monday – Saturday (daily percentage to be consumed)

20% complex carbs – 20% proteins – 30% vegetables and legumes – 15% fruits and nuts – 15% dairy foods and snacks

Or the equivalent in daily servings

Carbs (1-2 servings) – proteins (3-4 servings) – vegetables and legumes (3-6 servings) – Fruits and nuts (1.5-3 servings) – dairy foods and snacks (1.5 servings)

Sunday

(Some athletes don't train on Sundays or once a week so one day per week the food servings will change. We are using Sunday as that day.)

15% carbs – 25% proteins – 20% vegetables and legumes – 20% fruits and nuts – 20% dairy foods and snacks

Or the equivalent in servings

Carbs (1.5-3 servings) – proteins (2.5-3 servings) – vegetables and legumes (2 Servings) – Fruits and nuts (2-3 servings) – dairy foods and Snacks (2 servings)

*The percentages shown are for the daily consumption of these food groups and the servings are for the maximum amount of times you are allowed to consume these food groups. Follow the food group charts provided at the beginning of the book as a guide to what you can eat except for the dairies which you are free to choose the type and amount due to the variety of preferences and medical conditions out there.

<u>*Nutritional Guide for M C L A's*</u>

Monday - Saturday

15% carbs – 30% proteins – 25% vegetables and legumes – 15% fruits and nuts – 15% dairy foods and snacks

Or the equivalent in daily servings

Carbs (1.5-3 servings) – proteins (3-6 servings) – vegetables and legumes (2.5-6 servings) – Fruits and nuts (1.5-3 servings) – dairy foods and snacks (1.5-3 servings)

Sunday

(Some athletes don't train on Sundays or once a week so one day per week the food servings will change. We are using Sunday as that day.)

25% carbs – 20 % proteins – 20% vegetables and legumes – 20% fruits and nuts – 15% dairy foods and snacks

Or the equivalent in servings

Carbs (2.5-3 servings) – proteins (2-5 servings) – vegetables and legumes (2 servings) – Fruits and nuts (2 servings) – dairy foods and snacks (1.5 servings)

The percentages shown are for the daily consumption of these food groups and the servings are for the maximum amount of times you are allowed to consume these food groups. Follow the food group charts provided at the beginning of the book as a guide to what you can eat except for the dairies which you are free to choose the type and amount due to the variety of preferences and medical conditions out there.

Nutritional Guide for H C L A's

Monday - Saturday

20% carbs – 25% proteins – 20% vegetables and legumes – 15% fruits and nuts – 20% dairy foods and snacks

Or the equivalent in daily servings

Carbs (2 servings) – proteins (2.5 servings) – vegetables and legumes (2 servings) – Fruits and nuts (1.5 servings) – dairy foods and snacks (2 servings)

Sunday

(Some athletes don't train on Sundays or once a week so one day per week the food servings will change. We are using Sunday as that day.)

25% carbs – 20% proteins – 15% vegetables and legumes – 20% fruits and nuts – 20% dairy foods and snacks

Or the equivalent in servings

Carbs (2.5 servings) – proteins (2 servings) – vegetables and legumes (1.5 servings) – Fruits and nuts (2 servings) – dairy foods and snacks (2 servings)

*The percentages shown are for the daily consumption of these food groups and the servings are for the maximum amount of times you are allowed to consume these food groups. Follow the food group charts provided at the beginning of the book as a guide to what you can eat except for the dairies which you are free to choose the type and amount due to the variety of preferences and medical conditions out there.

CHAPTER 2

RESTING YOUR WAY TO A LEANER BODY

Your Secret Weapon RMR

RMR is also known as resting metabolic rate and is the number of calories burned while your body is at rest because of normal body functions such as the heart rate and the breathing function. This accounts for 75% of the total calories burned during the day. This can vary from one person to another depending on age, amount of fat in your body, and other factors. The less fat you have in your body and the more muscle you have the higher the RMR will be and the faster you will burn calories at rest, even in your sleep. This is what some people consider as having a good metabolism but it really equates to having a high RMR. Having a high RMR will make you leaner and make easier for you to stay leaner every day. How to do you accomplish this? You can do this by changing what you eat to reduce fats and sugars, and by adding muscle to your body.

Each and every day is an opportunity to get back in shape. When you're tired of work and constantly busy with all the tedious things in life, you stop thinking about the importance of taking care of your body and mind. For this reason, I have prepared a daily schedule to help you <u>get in shape all day even while you eat, sleep, and breathe.</u> How is this possible? You can do this by simply by accelerating your metabolism. A natural way of doing this is by making small changes in your life that have an immediate effect on your body.

This daily schedule can be changed to accommodate your lifestyle as well as your training schedule. <u>Things you already do on a normal day will be highlighted in bold just to remind you that you're not really changing your day to day schedule at all.</u>

Remember, you are the only one that can keep yourself motivated enough to go through with the schedule. Working out every day and sticking to this nutrition guide requires sacrifice and being able to let go of temptations.

Temptations

Every day we pass by a pastry shop or a vending machine full of goodies. These are the moments you have to stay strong. Look away! Think of something else. Think of work. Think of your family. Think of how hard you're working to get and stay in shape. There's no one to stop you from eating a donut or a soft drink or potato chips, it's up to you to be disciplined. Every time you're able to withstand temptation, you'll be that much stronger. In case you've never done this before, don't go to the grocery store on an empty stomach as you will definitely buy things you should not be eating.

Stop smoking

Smoking WILL lower your life expectancy and more importantly it WILL decrease your quality of life! This nutrition guide should be used to improve your longevity and performance as an athlete through physical exercise and improved nutrition. Smoking will work against you and your goals to improve your health habits.

Consume less alcohol

Drinking alcohol will dehydrate you much faster than most any other drinks so it would not be recommended you add this to your nutrition plan. Consult with your doctor to find out just how much is enough for you.

Improving your breathing techniques

Static breathing exercises, Yoga, Pilates, stretching, and other forms of breathing exercises will help you reduce your stress levels.

Less stress = A longer life

These exercises are for both men and women. They have changed my life and I am sure they will do the same for you. These are just some of the benefits you will see:

- Increased flexibility
- Stronger back and core muscles
- Improved posture
- Reduced stress

The Ideal Nutrition and Workout Schedule

Monday - Friday

7:00 AM   Drink one glass of water when you *wake up*.

7:15 AM   Complete a minimum of 5 abdominal exercises or 5 stretching exercises.

8:00 AM   Drink a glass of water, milk, or juice and then *eat breakfast*. Base your breakfast on the diet plan explained in chapter 1.

8:30 AM   Train as you normally would on a weekday.

10:00 AM   Drink one glass of water.

11:00 AM   Eat a fruit along with a multigrain bar (or another snack based on the list provided in chapter 1.). You can add or replace it with a yogurt or slices of a protein (turkey, ham, roast beef, fish, poultry, etc.).

11:10 AM   After having your snack make sure to take a 5 minute break to stretch and breathe, or simply relax your body so that you prepare your body for lunch in a peaceful environment.

2:00 PM   Drink a glass of water, juice, milk or other liquid and then *have lunch*.

2:45 PM   Rest at least 30 minutes to 1 hour to allow your body to fully digest the food.

4:00 PM   Start your afternoon training which might include going to the gym or simply resting if your morning training was enough.

5:00 PM	Complete abdominal exercises.

6:30 PM   Drink a glass of water, milk, or juice before *having dinner*. Remember to eat only foods explained in the nutrition plan in the first chapter.

8:30 PM   Eat a snack if your still hungry. Make sure to eat small quantities. <u>Remember that after dark you do not eat any carbs, fruits or foods that contain either one.</u>

10:00 PM   You should drink at least one glass of water before going to *sleep even if you sleep earlier or later than the time provided*.

Note:

You can adjust the schedule and the exercises as long as all the steps are completed and are in order. Also, make sure you stay within the 3 hour time difference between meals and drink a minimum of 6 – 8 glasses of water before the end of the day.

Improving the quality of events in your life and daily schedule will help you lose weight even while you are sleeping as your metabolism will accelerate at a faster rate and will move its way to your sleeping hours.

Saturday

For Saturday's schedule we are simply going to replace the time at work with time at home, entertainment, or doing some chores. Saturday would look something like this:

7:00 AM	Drink one glass of water when you *wake up*.
7:15 AM	Do a 5 minute morning stretch to get your muscles relaxed and ready for the day ahead.
8:00 AM	Drink a glass of water, milk, or juice and then *eat breakfast*. Base your breakfast on the diet plan explained in chapter 1.
8:30 AM	Train as you normally would on a weekday.
10:00 AM	Drink one glass of water.

11:00 AM	Eat a fruit along with a multigrain bar (or another snack based on the list provided in chapter 1.). You can add or replace it with a yogurt or slices of a protein (turkey, ham, roast beef, fish, poultry, etc.).
11:10 AM	After having your snack make sure to take a 5 minute break to stretch and breathe, or simply relax your body so that you prepare your body for lunch in a peaceful environment.
2:00 PM	Drink a glass of water, juice, milk or other liquid and then *have lunch*.
2:45 PM	Rest
5:30 PM	Drink a glass of water, milk, or juice before *having dinner*. Remember to eat only foods in

the nutrition guide provided at the beginning of this book.

8:30 PM	Eat a small meal and include a glass of water with this meal.
10:00 PM	Drink a glass of water before going to *sleep*.

CHAPTER 3

GET IN SHAPE ALL DAY LONG

Accelerating your metabolism to enhance performance

What you do if I told you that you could get in shape 24 hours a day? Sound impossible? Let me tell you how to do it through a very simple process that might surprise you in a sense because of its simplicity but first we will focus on the three main components of staying in shape and losing weight. They are: Patience, repetition, and focus.

Patience

It takes time to gain weight. Some people spend a year or more increasing their weight without ever controlling it. Dropping all that weight that has taken so long to accumulate takes time if you want lasting results. Let me repeat that one more time because it's a difficult concept to understand. It takes time to drop all the weight you have accumulated over the years. If you want quick results just work smarter and improve your nutrition. If you lose weight fast, be sure that it will come back just as fast if you don't continue to do what you did to drop it. *Don't fall for the easy way out* because it won't last and you'll be right back where you started. Be patient as small decreases in weight are more valuable in the long run than large ones that come right back. Your body will gradually adjust to the exercise routines and the nutritional plan. That means you will be building off your new results each time. Just be patient.

Over time your body weight works like a seesaw.

Your weight will increase as time goes by if you don't take the necessary steps to maintain it at a healthy level and it will decrease as time goes by if you work hard to control it. Maintaining your body weight is a matter of balance between nutrition and exercise.

Repetition

Changing your lifestyle takes time and it takes permanent decisions. If you decide to start working out but find yourself training once a week or every other week, then you obviously know what type of results you will have. You've got to be consistent. Also, you need to be repetitive in what you, from the first day of the month until the last day of the month. It sounds like a lot of work, but you have to realize that you already do a lot of things in a consistent manner that you might not have noticed. Do you eat at least three times a day, every day of every month of the year? <u>Do you watch TV at least an hour every day of every month?</u> Do you change your clothes every day of every month of the year? And do you take a shower every day of every month of the year? If you answered "yes" to these questions, it means you do a lot of things in a consistent way. I bet a lot of people never even realize they do all these things every day. It's definitely something you should use to your advantage, by simply adding some exercises and an effective diet plan to these everyday activities.

There are "quick fixes" that can get you where you want to be but most of the time they'll have some sort of side effect or health risk involved. That's not what this book is about. You're working on obtaining <u>long term results that will last</u> and that will eventually become a part of your life. That's why it's important to stick to these exercises and allow them to become a part of your daily life.

The most important thing is to be consistent if you want long term results so stay focused on getting there.

Focus

Focus is the art of being able to concentrate on something for a determined period of time. That's what I want you to do with your new exercise routine and dietary plan. Stay focused no matter what. Stay focused on the objective at hand. Stay focused on your new lifestyle. Work at it every day because it's your life and it's up to you and no one else to make it better.

Get in shape all day long

We spoke about increasing your RMR in the last chapter but now let's go into more detail.

Step 1: Start doing more exercise, preferably the exercises that involve increasing the amount of muscle in your body. Your body will to have to regenerate muscle tissue during the night time and this will contribute towards burning more energy. By doing this, you will lose weight and get fitter during the entire day!

Step 2: Follow the nutritional instructions described in chapter 1. Eating better and at scheduled times will change the short and long term effects your body and mind will have over time by reducing fat and simple sugar intake. This will help you to have a better defense mechanism that in turn will prevent you from getting sick or injured. It will boost your energy levels as well as help prevent future health problems such as obesity and heart disease. This is just to name a few of the most common ailments affecting our society today.

Step 3: Non-athletes need to drink a minimum of 6 to 8 glasses of water during the day, <u>especially one glass upon waking up and one before going to sleep.</u> As an athlete you should drink 6-10 glasses of water.

The Right Way to Drink Water

Water intake before the exercise, during the exercise and after the exercise should be properly planned.

A) Before training or competition consume 14-18 ounces of water two hours before any exercise. The two hour gap is enough to fully hydrate the body and leave enough time for excess water to come out of the system.

Take 5-7 ounces of water just 15 minutes before training.

B) During training or competition an athlete must constantly keep hydrating the body every 20-25 minutes with 5-10 ounces of water. Sports drinks are good sources of sodium which needs to be replenished in competition but should be mixed with some water to dilute the high sugar content they usually have to make them taste good.

Athletes who perspire excessively should consume 1.5 g of sodium and 2.3 g of chloride each day (or 3.8 g of salt) to replace the amount lost through perspiration. The maximum amount should not exceed 5.8 g of salt each day (2.3 g of sodium). Consult with your doctor if you have any of these medical conditions: elevated blood pressure, coronary heart disease, diabetes, and kidney disease, etc. These athletes should avoid consuming salt at the upper level. Endurance athletes and other individuals who are involved in strenuous activities are allowed to consume more sodium to offset sweat losses. The carbonates in the sports drinks also help the muscles perform better. Athletes should also have an adequate intake of 4.7 g of potassium per day to blunt the effects of salt, lower blood pressure, and reduce the risk of kidney stones and bone loss. Athletes should also eat foods rich in potassium such as bananas and prunes.

C) After training or competition an athlete should replace all lost fluids by drinking approximately 20 ounces of fluid for every pound of weight lost.

Step 4: Sleep at least 5 hours but no more than 10 per day and take power naps during the day if you feel you need to get more rest. Sleeping allows your body to recover from the wear and tear you experience every day. It's also a good time for your body to recover so that you can continue training the following day. Sleeping is an excellent way to relieve your body and mind of any excess stress that has accumulated during the day. Sleeping is important so make sure you get adequate hours of sleep every night.

Step 5: Working your cardiovascular endurance is a great way to accelerate your metabolism which will also strengthen your heart. Make sure you do as much aerobic exercise as possible without getting injured. Besides static exercises and stretching, aerobic exercises will provide you with one of the most important tools you can have towards having a higher resting metabolic rate which we talked about in the last chapter. Some good aerobic exercises you can do to cross train are: running, swimming, jumping, roller-blading, skiing, rowing, karate, and playing sports that require any combination of these. A good cardiovascular exercise you can do after lunch is walk up and down stairs at a slow pace and at a low intensity level. If you work or live in a building that has stairs, make sure you take advantage of this. A building with two floors would be sufficient since you can go up and down the same steps. Make sure you do this for at least 5 minutes to make it worthwhile. After eating, always try to do some form of low-intensity aerobic exercise besides walking up and down stairs. This might be one of the most important changes you make towards improving your overall health and fitness.

Our goal in this chapter is to naturally accelerate your metabolism by staying as active as possible during most of the day which will increase your RMR. A faster metabolism helps your body stay lean and fit but you want to make sure you do this naturally (without the use of artificial substances) and gradually so that these changes are easily maintained in months and years to come.

A SIMPLE EXPLANATION ON LOSING, GAINING, AND MAINTAINING BODY WEIGHT

Losing, gaining, and maintaining weight is all about simple math. If you consume 1 unit of food and exercise 1 unit, you will have a simple mathematical equation that looks like this:

$$1 - 1 = 0$$

Meaning, if you exercise the same amount you eat (unit wise) you should gain little or no weight.

Now, if you consume 1 unit of food and exercise "0" units, you will have an equation that looks like this:

$$1 - 0 = 1$$

Meaning, you will have gained "1" unit of weight. (I use the term "unit" to simplify things but it refers to the amount of weight.) This simply means that every day that you eat and don't exercise, you gain weight because you have a surplus.

Last, if you consume "1" unit of food and exercise "2" units, you will have an equation that will look like this:

$$1 - 2 = -1$$

Meaning, you have lost one unit of weight.

Important note: Not consuming any units of food (not eating) is not an option because this will create more harm than good. Instead of achieving your goals you will be delaying them and even causing irreversible health problems. You need food to survive. It is a basic necessity of life.

WHAT DOES THIS ALL MEAN?

The amount and quality of exercise you do will determine if you lose, gain, or maintain weight. Depending on what your goals are, this can actually make your life healthier. Just make sure to follow a nutritional plan that is right for you and your lifestyle. Refer to chapter 1 for more information on what you should be eating and how much of it. Warning! Do not go to extremes. Some people get sick by going on extreme diets that can ultimately create more harm than benefit. Below are some examples of extremes you want to avoid:

EXAMPLE 1

By eating simple sugars and fats, and NOT consuming food with nutritional value will reduce your potential performance outcome and will lower your quality of health in years to come. A balanced diet is necessary to stay fit. Even though this would not be considered an extreme diet it is still suggested that you stay away from prepackaged and canned foods, as well as foods with high fat content not derived from natural sources. Natural sources of fat would be avocado, nuts, olive oil, etc. and these are good for you but in the right proportions.

EXAMPLE 2

If you are an athlete that does a lot of cardio exercise and don't consume any carbohydrates such as bread, rice, and pasta. It can seriously affect your performance as well as your wellbeing. Cutting carbs completely out of your diet might not be a wise decision. If this is the case, you should consume some form of carbohydrate during the day to maintain the right energy reserves your body needs. You can still control your body weight but you have to consume at least a minimum of nutrients from a variety of food groups and this includes carbohydrates.

EXAMPLE 3

Eating a lot and not exercising. This is what this book focuses on preventing. This book will definitely help you to get fitter and improve the shape of your body into the body you've always wanted. Make it a priority to balance your nutritional life with everyday cardiovascular training.

EXAMPLE 4

Not sleeping enough can severely affect your mental and physical condition during training and competition. Sleeping allows you to recover and perform better in all aspects of your life. Take the necessary steps to control the amount and quality of your sleep.

CHAPTER 4

BETTER MARATHON PERFORMANCE THROUGH ANTIOXIDANTS

Change your nutritional lifestyle now to get long term results and faster recovery times

A number of elements in our body such as sunlight and pollution in our environment produce oxidation leading to the production of dangerous chemical compounds called free radicals. Free radicals can lead to serious cellular damage, which is the common pathway for cancer, ageing, and a variety of other diseases. Free radicals are highly reactive and pose a major threat by reacting with cell membranes in chain reactions leading to the death of the cells. Antioxidants are molecules that can help in destroying the free radicals so that the body can be free from the dangers associated with the free radicals. Moreover, athletes should have a keen interest in them because of health concerns and the prospect of enhanced performance and/or recovery after exercise. The way antioxidants work is that they can react with the free radicals and shut down the chain reaction leading to the death of the DNA cells and thus save them.

The main sources of antioxidants are:

1. Vitamin E: It is an antioxidant and helps protect cells from damage. It is also important for the health of red blood cells. Vitamin E is found in many foods such as vegetable oils, nuts, and leafy green vegetables. Avocados, wheat germ, and whole grains are also good sources of this vitamin.

2. Beta-carotene: It is a precursor to vitamin A (retinol) and is present in liver, egg yolk, milk, butter, spinach, carrots, tomatoes, and grains.

3. Vitamin C: It is needed to form collagen, a tissue that helps in holding cells together. It is essential for healthy bones, teeth, gums, and blood vessels. It helps the body absorb iron and calcium, aids in wound healing, and contributes to brain function. You will find high levels of vitamin C in red berries, kiwifruit, red and green bell peppers, tomatoes, broccoli, spinach, and juices made from guava, grapefruit, and orange.

4. Selenium: It is a trace element and is also an important antioxidant.

Some Popular Antioxidants are Mentioned Below:

Strengthening our immune system will help you absorb antioxidants and protect you from free radicals which can be done through exercise. That's why a combination of cardiovascular and weight training in combination with added antioxidants in your diet will improve you performance and allow you to have less low energy or sick days. By consuming more antioxidants your recovery phase will be faster which will allow you to compete sooner than normal.

Project the Right Image through a

Better Posture to Win More

Studies have shown that athletes who project a strong positive image are prone to being more successful and have a stronger immune system. Having a strong immune system will keep you healthier and prone to less injuries which equates to having the prospect of winning more simply because you can compete more often.

 Definitive change from the caveman era to now is our posture. For some reason a lot of athletes look like they are back in the caveman era. Maybe some athletes have this hunched posture because they don't work on flexibility and back strengthening exercises or maybe because of lack of confidence. Whatever may be the reason, an athlete's posture says a lot about how they feel and what they project specially to their competition. Showing a lack of confidence to your competition will only motivate them to do better. To succeed more as an athlete start showing more confidence through a better posture even when you are not competing.

Most of us forget that as we get older our backs hunch even more and it becomes more difficult to stay straight. I would rather work on having a better posture now than later because later might never come. I forgot to mention that not standing up straight makes you look fatter as well. So if you want to start looking thinner, start standing up straight! For this and many other reasons, it's essential to focus on your posture.

It has often been overlooked by many but can help you get to a better figure faster than you can imagine. Did you know that by walking in a slouched position you are actually making your stomach muscles lazier and thus promoting that shape of abdominal muscles? Not a good habit to have. By walking straight you are actually working your abs.

Posture is a matter of habit

You must concentrate on maintaining a straight posture all the time. Focus on keeping a good posture when you walk, when you sit and when you stand. Posture is also very important when you eat because it helps food pass through your digestive system easier than if you were slouched. Chewing your food better can contribute to the reduction or better yet, prevention, of digestion or acid reflux related issues.

Also, *consider that no matter how hard you work and how good a body you may have, if you slouch, you just ruined the picture (the image of yourself and what you project to others) and made all that effort become almost unnoticed.* For this specific reason, I want to remind you how vital it is to concentrate, work on and make a habit of standing, sitting and walking with a straight posture.

Key points to having a better posture are:

1. Your Shoulders should be relaxed and below your neck height.
2. Your Chest should be out and shoulders back.
3. Your Head needs to be perpendicular to the ground. (Imagine drawing a straight line from your chin to the ground.)
4. Your Eyes should be focused on the horizon NOT on the ground.

CHAPTER 5

High Protein Calendar

Planning for success one day at a time

These meals will help increase muscle in an organized manner by adding large healthy portions of protein to your diet. Being too busy to eat right can sometimes become a problem and that's why this book will save you time and help nourish your body to achieve the goals you want. Make sure you know what you're eating by preparing it yourself or having someone prepare it for you.

DAY	BREAKFAST	SNACK	LUNCH	SNACK	DINNER
1.	2 boiled eggs with chopped basil	1 grapefruit	1 beef sirloin with slices of eggplant	1 cup of tomato and walnuts salad	1 cup of cooked chard with olive oil
2.	½ cup of baked mushrooms with rosemary	1 pear	1 cup of octopus salad with tomatoes and capers	1 cup of roasted almonds	1 grilled zucchini with garlic and parsley
3.	1 glass of mixed fruits and vegetables shake	1 glass of fresh apricot juice	2 cups of fish stew	1 peach	1 cup of fresh fruits of your choice
4.	½ cup of pineapple omelette with almonds	1 orange	1 beef chop with pineapple and tumeric	1 cup of chopped cucumber with fennel	2 apples
5.	1 cup of fruit salad	1 cup of tuna salad with lettuce and curry	1 turkey drumstick with nutmeg and carob	3 grilled eggplant slices with chopped fennel	1 cup of octopus salad with tomatoes and capers
6.	1 cup of spinach omelet	1 glass of fresh pineapple juice without sugar	1 medium piece of eggplant casserole	1 cup of cooked leek with lemon sauce	2 boiled eggs with grated ginger
7.	1 cup of tomato and walnuts salad	1 cup of cooked mushrooms with vegetables and ginger sauce	3 chicken wings with tumeric sauce	1 cup of tomato and tuna salad	1 veal steak with red pepper sauce
8.	½ cup of mushroom omelet	1 glass of fresh cranberry juice	2 turkey fillet with walnuts and maple syrup	2 boiled eggs	1 cup of roasted cherry tomatoes, eggplant and basil salad
9.	½ cup of nutmeg omelet	1 cup of shrimps in tomato sauce	1 cup of lettuce salad	5 dried plums	1 cup of coriander salad
10.	2 fried eggs with chopped mint	1 cup of tuna salad with lettuce and curry	1 veal chop with chopped cloves	1 cup of tomato soup	2 boiled eggs with chopped coriander
11.	3 pineapple slices with grated almonds	1 grilled zucchini with chopped	1 cup of chopped veal soup	2 cooked carrots	1 cup of grapes

			basil and mint	with vegetables		
12.	1 cup of cooked broccoli	2 cups of fruit salad	1 lamb cutlet with hazelnut sauce	1 grilled red pepper	1 cooked potato in parsley sauce
13.	1 cup of eggplant pate	1 cup of lettuce and tuna salad	½ cup of stewed beef and cabbage	1 cup of broccoli soup	1 cup of roasted almonds
14.	1 glass of fresh orange juice	½ cup of walnuts	1 grilled trout fillets with parsley	1 cup of fresh cranberries and grated walnuts	1 cup of cauliflower soup
15.	½ cup of tomato omelet	1 cup of berries	1 grilled salmon fillet	2 carrots	1 cup of roasted almonds
16.	1 glass of fresh orange and lime juice	1 cup of mixed vegetable salad	1 cup of grilled calamari in curry sauce	3 fresh figs	2 grilled sardines
17.	1 glass of banana shake	2 grilled green peppers	1 cup of seafood salad	2 baked apples	1 grilled zucchini with garlic
18.	2 boiled eggs	1 pear and roasted almonds	1 grilled steak with pineapple slices	1 cup of cooked cauliflower in mint sauce	1 grated apple with walnuts and cinnamon
19.	1 cup of mushroom soup	1 trout fillet with almond and tumeric sauce	1 cup of trout soup	1 cup of cucumber salad	½ cup of grilled mushrooms with garlic sauce
20.	1 glass of fresh lime juice	2 cups of cooked, canned broccoli	1 beef chop with pineapple and tumeric	1 glass of fresh tomato juice	2 grilled sardines
21.	3 apple and carrot balls with cinnamon	1 grilled eggplant with parsley	1 cup of steak salad with mushrooms	1 cooked carrot	1 sour asparagus
22.	1 glass of fruit shake	3 grilled eggplant slices	1 veal cutlet with almonds	1 cup of berries and Brazil nuts	2 grilled red peppers
23.	½ cup of spinach omelet	1 cup tomato and garlic soup	2 squids stuffed with walnuts	1 glass of fresh lemonade	½ cup of Brazil nuts
24.	1 banana	1 cup of lettuce and tuna salad	1 lamb cutlet with basil	1 cucumber	1 cup of grilled mushrooms in tomato sauce

25.	2 fried eggs	½ cup of Brazil and Macadamia nuts	1 cup of shrimp skewers	1 cup of cooked broccoli	1 glass of fresh vegetable juice of your choice
26.	3 pineapple slices with grated almonds	1 cup of broccoli soup	2 turkey fillet with walnuts and maple syrup salmon in almond sauce	1 cup of lettuce and cherry tomato salad	1 apple
27.	1 glass of fresh carrot juice	1 cup of cucumber salad	1 beef chop with pineapple and tumeric	1 cup of chopped cucumber with fennel	1 cup of cooked leek with lemon sauce
28.	1 cup of tomato and walnuts salad	1 glass of fresh apricot juice	2 cups of fish stew	3 dried plums	1 cup of trout soup
29.	3 apple and carrot balls with cinnamon	1 grilled zucchini with chopped basil and mint	1 beef chop with pineapple and tumeric	1 cup of roasted almonds	1 cup of octopus salad with tomatoes and capers
30.	1 cup of eggplant pate	1 cup of cooked mushrooms with vegetables and ginger sauce	1 medium piece of eggplant casserole	1 glass of lemonade without sugar	1 cup of roasted cherry tomatoes, eggplant and basil salad

CHAPTER 6

High Protein Muscle Recipes

Easy to follow recipes to increase muscle

1. Boiled eggs with chopped basil

Ingredients:

2 eggs

1 tsp of chopped basil

pepper

Preparation:

Boil eggs for 10 minutes. Peel and chop into small pieces. Sprinkle with chopped basil.

Nutritional values per 100 g:

Carbohydrates 1.1g

Sugar 0g

Protein 13g

Total fat (good monounsaturated fat) 11g

Sodium 124mg

Potassium 126mg

Calcium 50mg

Iron 1.2mg

Vitamins (vitamin A; B-6; B-12; C)

Calories 155

2. Beef sirloin with slices of eggplant

Ingredients:

1 thin beef sirloin

1 medium eggplant

1 tsp of olive oil

chopped basil

pepper

Preparation:

Wash and pepper the meat. Grill it on a barbecue pan for about 10 minutes on each side. Remove from pan. Peel eggplant and cut two thick slices. Fry for few minutes in the same barbecue pan. Remove from heat and serve with beef. Sprinkle with chopped basil.

Nutritional values:

Carbohydrates 6g

Sugar 1.2g

Protein 35.2 g

Total fat 4.9g

Sodium 57 mg

Potassium 397mg

Calcium 18.5mg

Iron 1.9mg

Vitamins (vitamin A; B-6; B-12; C; D; D2; D3; K;Thiamin; K)

Calories 212

3. Tomato and walnuts salad

Ingredients:

1 big tomato

½ cup of chopped walnuts

1 tsp of lemon juice

Preparation:

Wash and cut tomato into small pieces. Add chopped walnuts and mix well. Pour lemon juice over it.

Nutritional values for 1 cup:

Carbohydrates 8.2g

Sugar 3.8g

Protein 10g

Total fat 4.5g

Sodium 17 mg

Potassium 112mg

Calcium 16.5mg

Iron 1.3mg

Vitamins (vitamin A; B-6; B-12; C; D; D2; D3; K; Riboflavin; Niacin; Thiamin; K)

Calories 218

4. Cooked chard with olive oil

Ingredients:

1 bunch of chard

1 tsp of olive oil

1 tsp of tumeric

Preparation:

Wash and chop chard. Fry it in olive oil for 20 minutes on a low temperature, or until tender. Add tumeric before serving.

Nutritional values for one cup:

Carbohydrates 6.9g

Sugar 2.1g

Protein 8.4 g

Total fat 1.9g

Sodium 34.2 mg

Potassium 23.2mg

Calcium 12.4mg

Iron 0.59mg

Vitamins (vitamin A; B-6; B-12; C; D; D2; D3; K; Riboflavin; Niacin; Thiamin; K)

Calories 113

5. Baked mushrooms with rosemary

Ingredients:

1 cup of mushrooms

1 tsp of olive oil

1 tsp of chopped rosemary

Preparation:

Bake mushrooms in a barbecue pan for 5-7 minutes. Remove from pan and sprinkle with olive oil and chopped rosemary.

Nutritional values for one cup:

Carbohydrates 6.2g

Sugar 1.1g

Protein 8.4 g

Total fat (good monounsaturated fat) 1.3g

Sodium 48.2 mg

Potassium 23.2mg

Calcium 12.4mg

Iron 0.59mg

Vitamins (vitamin A; B-6; B-12; C; D; D2; D3; K; Riboflavin; Niacin; Thiamin; K)

Calories 117

6. Octopus salad with tomatoes and capers

Ingredients:

1 cup of frozen cut octopus

¼ cup of capers

½ cup of olives

5 cherry tomatoes

1 tsp of chopped parsley

1 tsp of chopped celery

1 small onion

2 cloves of garlic

1 tsp of chopped rosemary

1 tbsp of olive oil

1 tsp of lemon juice

Preparation:

Cook the octopus in salted water until tender. It usually takes about 20-30 minutes. Remove from pot, wash and drain. Wash and cut vegetables and mix with octopus. Mix the spices and add to salad. Sprinkle with olive oil and lemon juice. Cool well before serving.

Nutritional values for one cup:

Carbohydrates 12.9g

Sugar 5.1g

Protein 16.4 g

Total fat (good monounsaturated fat) 9.9g

Sodium 114.2 mg

Potassium 83.2mg

Calcium 42.4mg

Iron 0.59mg

Vitamins (vitamin A; B-6; B-12; C; D; D2; D3; K; Riboflavin; Niacin; Thiamin; K)

Calories 81

7. Grilled zucchini with garlic and parsley

Ingredients:

1 medium zucchini

1 tbsp of chopped parsley

2 cloves of garlic

Preparation:

Peel the zucchini and cut into 4 slices. Fry in a barbecue pan for 3-4 minutes. Add chopped garlic and bake for another 5 minutes. Sprinkle with parsley before serving.

Nutritional values:

Carbohydrates 3.71g

Sugar 3g

Protein 2 g

Total fat 0g

Sodium 2.9 mg

Potassium 360mg

Calcium 0.2mg

Iron 0.3mg

Vitamins (vitamin A; B-6; B-12; C; D:K)

Calories 20

8. Mixed fruits and vegetables shake

Ingredients:

1 cup of mixed blueberries, raspberries, blackberries and strawberries

½ cup of chopped baby spinach

2 cups of water

Preparation:

Mix ingredients in a blender for few minutes.

Nutritional values for 1 cup:

Carbohydrates 9.2g

Sugar 6.15g

Protein 8.75g

Total fat 0.87g

Sodium 54.8mg

Potassium 107.8mg

Calcium 82mg

Iron 2.03mg

Vitamins (Vitamin C total ascorbic acid; B-6; B-12; Folate-DFE; A-RAE; A-IU; E-alpha-tocopherol; D; D-D2+D3; K-phylloquinone; Thianin; Riboflavin; Niacin)

Calories 42.6

9. Fish stew

Ingredients:

1 carp fillet

1 carrot

2 chili peppers

1 medium tomato

pepper

celery roots and leaf

Preparation:

It is the best to buy cooked carrots, or cook them before preparing the fish stew. Wash and cut vegetables, mix with celery and fish and put in a pot. Pour little water, just to cover it. Cook on a low temperature for 20-30 minutes.

Nutritional values:

Carbohydrates 8.2g

Sugar 3.9g

Protein 15.2 g

Total fat (good monounsaturated fat) 6.6g

Sodium 113.8 mg

Potassium 71mg

Calcium 29.1mg

Iron 0.32mg

Vitamins (vitamin A; B-6; B-12; C; D; D2; D3;
K; Riboflavin; Niacin; Thiamin; K)

Calories 172

10. Pineapple omelet with almonds

Ingredients:

3 slices of pineapple

2 eggs

½ cup of almonds

1 tbsp of flaxseed oil for frying

Preparation:

Beat the eggs and add almonds. Fry pineapple slices for few minutes on both sides, without oil. When done, remove from pan, add oil, heat it and add eggs mixture. Serve with baked pineapple slices.

Nutritional values per 100g:

Carbohydrates 8.9g

Sugar 4.6g

Protein 19.2 g

Total fat 13.6g

Sodium 134.8 mg

Potassium 131mg

Calcium 67.1mg

Iron 1.52mg

Vitamins (vitamin A; B-12; C; K; Riboflavin; Niacin; K)

Calories 187

11. Beef chop with pineapple and tumeric

Ingredients:

1 medium beef chop

1 tbsp of olive oil

1 tsp of tumeric

Pepper

2 pineapple slices

Preparation:

Wash and dry the meat. Fry it without oil, in it's own sauce, for 15-20 minutes on low temperature. Remove from heat. Make a sauce with olive oil, tumeric and pepper and spread it over fried beef. Fry it once more for 3-4 minutes, add pineapple slices and serve warm.

Nutritional values per 100g:

Carbohydrates 15.7g

Sugar 9.9g

Protein 34g

Total fat (good monounsaturated fat) 17.6g

Sodium 99.3 mg

Potassium 328mg

Calcium 49.1mg

Iron 0.52mg

Vitamins (vitamin A; B-6; B-12; C; D; D2; D3; K; Riboflavin; Niacin; Thiamin; K)

Calories 311

12. Fruit salad

Ingredients:

1 cup of berries

½ cup of pineapple cubes

½ cup of chopped apple

1 tsp of cinnamon

1 tsp of agave syrup

Preparation:

Mix fruits, add agave syrup and sprinkle with cinnamon.

Nutritional values for one cup:

Carbohydrates 19.2g

Sugar 12g

Protein 15.2 g

Total fat (good monounsaturated fat) 4.6g

Sodium 123.8 mg

Potassium 95mg

Calcium 44.1mg

Iron 0.52mg

Vitamins (vitamin A; B-6; B-12; C; D; D2; D3; K; Riboflavin; Niacin; Thiamin; K)

Calories 77

13. Tuna salad with lettuce and curry

Ingredients:

1 small can of tuna without oil

1 bunch of lettuce

2 chili peppers

1 tsp of curry

1 tsp of lemon sauce

Preparation:

Wash and cut lettuce. Mix it with tuna, add chopped chili peppers and lemon sauce. Sprinkle with curry.

Nutritional values for 1 cup:

Carbohydrates 23.4g

Sugar 13g

Protein 33.2g

Total fat (good monounsaturated fat) 12.4g

Sodium 123mg

Potassium 72.3mg

Calcium 42.1mg

Iron 0.27mg

Vitamins (vitamin A; B-6; B-12; C; D; D2; D3; K; Riboflavin; Niacin; Thiamin; K)

Calories 68

14. Turkey drumstick with nutmeg and carob

Ingredients:

1 turkey drumstick

½ cup of water

½ cup of nutmeg

½ cup of carob

Preparation:

Wash and clean the meat. Fry it for about 15 minutes in it's own sauce (add some water while frying the turkey). Finely chop nutmeg and carob and add to saucepan. Mix well with turkey sauce. Remove from the pan and sprinkle with some more carob.

Nutritional values for one cup:

Carbohydrates 3.2g

Sugar 0.9g

Protein 31g

Total fat (good monounsaturated fat) 10.4g

Sodium 998mg

Potassium 78.2mg

Calcium 48mg

Iron 0.37mg

Vitamins (vitamin A; B-6; B-12; C; D; D2; D3; K; Riboflavin; Niacin; Thiamin; K)

Calories 210

15. Grilled eggplant slices with chopped fennel

Ingredients:

1 large eggplant

½ cup of chopped fennel

1 tbsp of olive oil

1 tsp of chopped parsley

Preparation:

Peel the eggplant and cut into 3 slices. Bake it in a barbecue pan without oil. When done, spread olive oil over it, sprinkle with fennel and parsley.

(These eggplant slices are great cold, so you can leave them overnight in a refrigerator)

Nutritional values per slice:

Carbohydrates 8.9g

Sugar 3g

Protein 7g

Total fat (good monounsaturated fat) 2.4g

Sodium 54mg

Potassium 32.5mg

Calcium 12.4mg

Iron 0.37mg

Vitamins (vitamin A; B-6; B-12; C; D; D2; D3; K; Riboflavin; Niacin; Thiamin; K)

Calories 54

16. Spinach omelet

Ingredients:

1 cup of chopped spinach

2 eggs

1 tbsp of olive oil for frying

Preparation:

Cook spinach in salted water until tender. Remove from pan and drain. Fry in olive oil for 5-6 minutes and add eggs. Mix well and serve warm.

Nutritional values per 100g:

Carbohydrates 1.9g

Sugar 0.6g

Protein 19.2 g

Total fat 13.6g

Sodium 144mg

Potassium 133mg

Calcium 71mg

Iron 1.8mg

Vitamins (vitamin A; B-12; C; K; Riboflavin; Niacin; K)

Calories 177

17. Eggplant casserole

Ingredients:

2 large eggplants

1 cup of minced meat

1 medium onion

1 tsp of olive oil

pepper

2 medium tomatoes

1 tsp of chopped parsley

Preparation:

Peel the eggplants and cut lengthwise into thin sheets. Put them in a bowl, and leave them to sit for at least an hour. Roll them in beaten eggs. Fry in hot oil. Cut the onion, fry, add sliced peppers, tomato, which is cut into cubes, and finely chopped parsley. Fry for few minutes and then add the meat. When meat is tender, remove from heat, cool, add 1 egg and season with pepper. Put fried eggplant and meat with vegetables in an ovenproof dish and make layers until you have used all the material. Bake for 30 minutes at 300 degrees.

Nutritional values per 100g:

Carbohydrates 7.9g

Sugar 3.4g

Protein 10.2 g

Total fat 13.6g

Sodium 164mg

Potassium 302mg

Calcium 21.1mg

Iron 1.32mg

Vitamins (vitamin A; B-12; C; K; Riboflavin; Niacin; K)

Calories 109

18. Leek with chicken cubes

Ingredients:

2 cups of trimmed leeks

1 cup of chicken fillets, cut into cubes

olive oil

thyme leaves for decoration

salt to taste

Preparation:

Cut the leeks into small pieces and wash it under cold water, day before serving. Leave it overnight in a plastic bag.

Heat the oil in a large pan. Add chicken cubes and fry for about 15 minutes on a medium temperature. Add leaks, mix well and fry for another 10 minutes on a low temperature. Remove from the saucepan and allow it to cool. Decorate with thyme leaves.

Nutritional values for 1 cup:

Carbohydrates 7g

Sugar 1.6g

Protein 18.1 g

Total fat 13.6g

Sodium 124.1 mg

Potassium 120mg

Calcium 69.3mg

Iron 1.42mg

Vitamins (vitamin A; B-6; B-12; C; D; D2; D3; K; Riboflavin; Niacin; Thiamin; K)

Calories 187

19. Cooked mushrooms with vegetables

Ingredients:

2 cups of button mushrooms

1cup of dried turkey cubes

2 large carrots

½ cup of chopped cabbage

1 tsp of ginger

1 tbsp of olive oil

1 tsp of chopped parsley

Preparation:

Cook vegetables in water until tender. Remove from pan and drain. Allow it to cool for a while. Mix olive oil, ginger and parsley, add little water and cook it for few minutes, on a medium heat. Pour over vegetables, add dried turkey and mix well. Allow it to cool in the refrigerator for about 30 minutes before serving.

Nutritional values for 1 cup:

Carbohydrates 18.6g

Sugar 11.3g

Protein 21.9g

Total fat 14.2g

Sodium 153.3 mg

Potassium 89.8mg

Calcium 49.9mg

Iron 0.42mg

Vitamins (vitamin A; B-6; B-12; C; D; D2; D3; K; Riboflavin; Niacin; Thiamin; K)

Calories 79

20. Chicken wings with tumeric sauce

Ingredients:

2 chicken wings

1 tsp of tumeric

1 tbsp of olive oil

½ tsp of dried rosemary

¼ tsp of red pepper

Preparation:

Fry chicken wings in a barbecue pan for 10-15 minutes. 3-4 minutes before chicken is done, add olive oil, tumeric, rosemary, pepper and a little water. Mix well the sauce and soak the chicken in it.

Nutritional values per 100g:

Carbohydrates 18.6g

Sugar 0.9g

Protein 28g

Total fat 22.7g

Sodium 431.3 mg

Potassium 189mg

Calcium 2.9mg

Iron 2.42mg

Vitamins (vitamin A; B-6; B-12; C; D; D2; D3; K; Riboflavin; Niacin; Thiamin; K)

Calories 318

21. Tomato and tuna salad

Ingredients:

2 large tomatoes

2 medium onions

3 cans of tuna

1 tbsp of olive oil

1 tsp of lemon juice

basil

salt to taste

Preparation:

Wash and peel the vegetables. Cut it into small cubes. Add olive oil, lemon juice and basil. Mix well.

Nutritional values for one cup:

Carbohydrates 17.9g

Sugar 9.1g

Protein 28.3 g

Total fat (good monounsaturated fat) 15.8g

Sodium 127mg

Potassium 89.6mg

Calcium 42.1mg

Iron 0.38mg

Vitamins (vitamin A; B-6; B-12; C; D; D2; D3; K; Riboflavin; Niacin; Thiamin; K)

Calories 99

22. Veal steak with red pepper sauce

Ingredients:

1 medium veal steak

1 large red paprika

1 tsp of red pepper

1 tbsp of olive oil

chopped rosemary

Preparation:

Wash and cut paprika into small pieces. Put in a large pan, add olive oil and rosemary. Stew for 15 minutes on low heat. Add red pepper and cook for another few minutes. Wash and dry the steak. Fry it in a barbecue pan until tender. Add sauce and remove from pan.

Nutritional values per 100g:

Carbohydrates 4.5g

Sugar 2.1g

Protein 26 g

Total fat 9.8g

Sodium 87 mg

Potassium 339mg

Calcium 2.1mg

Iron 0.16mg

Vitamins (vitamin A; B-6; B-12; C; D; D2; D3; K)

Calories 203

23. Mushroom omelet

Ingredients:

1 cup of mushrooms,

2 eggs

1 tbsp of olive oil

Preparation:

Fry the mushrooms in olive oil on a low temperature. Let the mushroom sauce evaporate. Add eggs and mix well.

Nutritional values per 100 g:

Carbohydrates 4.1g

Sugar 0g

Protein 18g

Total fat (good monounsaturated fat) 11g

Sodium 126mg

Potassium 124mg

Calcium 14.9mg

Iron 1.8mg

Vitamins (vitamin A; B-6; B-12; C)

Calories 174

24. Turkey fillet with walnuts and maple syrup

Ingredients:

3 turkey fillets

½ cup of walnuts

1 tsp of maple syrup

¼ cup of water

1 tbsp of olive oil

salt to taste

Preparation:

Fry the fillets in a barbecue pan on a low temperature for about 15 minutes, or until tender. Remove from the heath and add water, maple syrup and walnuts. Mix well and fry for another 5-6 minutes until the water evaporates. Allow it to cool for a while.

Nutritional values per 100 g:

Carbohydrates 10.1g

Sugar 7.3g

Protein 24.2g

Total fat 8.7g

Sodium 1025mg

Potassium 126mg

Calcium 50mg

Iron 1.2mg

Vitamins (vitamin A; B-6; C)

Calories 148

25. Roasted cherry tomatoes, eggplant and basil salad

Ingredients:

1 small eggplant

5 egg whites

1 cup of cherry tomatoes

1 tsp of fresh chopped basil

1 tbsp of olive oil

white pepper to taste

1 tsp of lemon juice

Preparation:

Cut eggplant into thick pieces, dice shape. Salt the eggplant cubes, add oil, egg whites and place on a baking sheet. If necessary, add some more olive oil (this is optional). Bake for about 10 minutes in preheated oven at 350 degrees. Clean the cherry tomatoes and fry for about 15 minutes on a low temperature, using a small saucepan. You want to get lightly caramelized tomato sauce. Remove from the heath and allow it to cool for a while. Gently stir in the lemon sauce, olive oil and fresh basil. Pour over the eggplant and serve cold. A great side dish with barbecue or grilled fish. You can keep it in the fridge up to one week.

Nutritional values per slice:

Carbohydrates 10.4g

Sugar 3g

Protein 19g

Total fat (good monounsaturated fat) 4.9g

Sodium 52mg

Potassium 38.3mg

Calcium 12.9mg

Iron 0.32mg

Vitamins (vitamin A; B-6; B-12; C; D; D2; D3; K; Riboflavin; Niacin; Thiamin; K)

Calories 87

26. Nutmeg omelet

Ingredients:

3 eggs

2 tbsp of olive oil

1 tsp of nutmeg

1/5 tsp of pepper

Preparation:

Beat the eggs and add nutmeg and pepper. Mix well and fry in olive oil for few minutes. Serve warm. You can add some salt if you like.

Nutritional values per 100g:

Carbohydrates 0.9g

Sugar 0.45g

Protein 12g

Total fat 12.4g

Sodium 156mg

Potassium 117.5mg

Calcium 4.4mg

Iron 7.37mg

Vitamins (vitamin A; B-6; D; D2; D3)

Calories 156

27. Shrimps in tomato sauce

Ingredients:

2 cups of frozen shrimps

1 large tomato

1 tsp of dried basil

2 cloves of garlic

3 tbsp of olive oil

salt to taste

Preparation:

Grill frozen shrimps in a barbecue pan without oil. Wash and cut tomato into small pieces, add chopped basil, chopped garlic and olive oil. Cook it for 5-6 minutes (add some water if necessary). Pour the sauce over the grilled shrimps. Serve with lettuce.

Nutritional values per 100g:

Carbohydrates 7.9g

Sugar 4.2g

Protein 28g

Total fat (good monounsaturated fat) 1.32g

Sodium 131mg

Potassium 269.5mg

Calcium 8.7mg

Iron 4.37mg

Vitamins (vitamin A; B-6; B-12; C; D; D2; D3; K; Riboflavin; Niacin; Thiamin; K)

Calories 164

28. Lettuce salad

Ingredients:

1 bunch of lettuce

1 tbsp of olive oil

1 tsp of lemon juice

Preparation:

Wash and cut the lettuce, add olive oil and lemon juice. It is the best to prepare this salad before serving a meal. Don't let it stand long.

Nutritional values per 1 cup:

Carbohydrates 1.2g

Sugar 0.3g

Protein 1.7g

Total fat (good monounsaturated fat) 1.4g

Sodium 19mg

Potassium 132mg

Calcium 1.4mg

Iron 2.3mg

Vitamins (vitamin A; B-6; B-12; C;K)

Calories 25

29. Coriander salad

Ingredients:

1 cup of chopped coriander

1 boiled egg

2 cups of cherry tomatoes

1 tsp of tumeric

2 tbsp of olive oil

1 tsp of lemon sauce

salt to taste

Preparation:

Wash and cut cherry tomatoes and mix with coriander. Add tumeric, olive oil and lemon sauce.

Nutritional values for one cup:

Carbohydrates 14.2g

Sugar 8.9g

Protein 10g

Total fat (good monounsaturated fat) 9.6g

Sodium 122.2 mg

Potassium 81mg

Calcium 45.5mg

Iron 0.37mg

Vitamins (vitamin A; B-6; B-12; C; D; D2; D3; K; Riboflavin; Niacin; Thiamin; K)

Calories 55

30. Fried eggs with chopped mint

Ingredients:

3 eggs

1 tbsp of olive oil

1 tbsp of chopped mint

1 cup of cherry tomatoes

1 small onion

pepper to taste

salt to taste

Preparation:

Cut the vegetables into small pieces and fry in large saucepan on a low temperature for about 15 minutes. Wait for the water to evaporate. Beat the eggs and add chopped mint. Mix with vegetables, add olive oil and fry for few minutes. Before serving add some salt and pepper to taste.

Nutritional values per 100 g:

Carbohydrates 8.1g

Sugar 4g

Protein 28g

Total fat (good monounsaturated fat) 11.9g

Sodium 176mg

Potassium 174mg

Calcium 17.9mg

Iron 1.5mg

Vitamins (vitamin A; B-6; B-12; C; D; D2; D3; K; Riboflavin; Niacin; Thiamin; K)

Calories 194

31. Veal chop with chopped cloves

Ingredients:

2 large veal chops

1 cup of chopped cloves

4 tbsp of olive oil

1 tbsp of dried parsley

1 tsp of rosemary

1 tsp of red pepper

1 tbsp of lemon juice

Preparation:

Mix well the cloves, olive oil, parsley and rosemary to get a nice sauce. Wash the steak and put it in a small baking tray. Add sauce and bake for 15-20 minutes at 300 degrees. Remove from the oven, sprinkle with pepper and lemon juice. Decorate with few parsley leaves. Allow it to cool for about 10 minutes.

Nutritional values per 100g:

Carbohydrates 8.2g

Sugar 4.9g

Protein 22g

Total fat 9.6g

Sodium 97.2 mg

Potassium 381mg

Calcium 4.5mg

Iron 5.3mg

Vitamins (vitamin A; B-6; B-12; C; D; D2; D3; K; Riboflavin; Niacin; Thiamin; K)

Calories 216

32. Tomato soup

Ingredients:

1 cup of tomato sauce

2 egg whites

2 cups of water

2 cloves of garlic

2 tbsp of olive oil

1tsp of dried marjoram

chopped parsley

Preparation:

Fry finely chopped garlic in oil. Stir in tomato sauce mixed with water. Add parsley and let it boil. Serve with marjoram.

Nutritional values per 150ml:

Carbohydrates 6.8g

Sugar 3.9g

Protein 7g

Total fat (good monounsaturated fat) 0.6g

Sodium 190.2 mg

Potassium 112mg

Calcium 0.5mg

Iron 2.3mg

Vitamins (vitamin A; C)

Calories 30

33. Grilled zucchini with chopped basil and mint

Ingredients:

1 large zucchini

¼ cup of chopped basil

¼ cup of chopped mint

1 tbsp of olive oil

¼ glass of water,

pepper to taste

Preparation:

Cook spices in water and add pepper for 2-3 minutes. Peel and cut zucchini into three slices. Grill it in a barbecue pan with olive oil. Add mint and basil. Fry until all the water evaporates. You can add some lemon juice before serving, but this is optional.

Nutritional values for 1 slice:

Carbohydrates 3.8g

Sugar 2g

Protein 2.9 g

Total fat 0.9g

Sodium 2.76 mg

Potassium 343mg

Calcium 0.27mg

Iron 0.3mg

Vitamins (vitamin A; B-6; B-12; C; D:K)

Calories 23

34. Chopped veal soup with vegetables

Ingredients:

1 thick veal steak

2 large carrots

½ cup of chopped parsley

1 large tomato

¼ tsp of pepper

1 small onion

Preparation:

Wash the meat and put it in a pot. Pour water and cook until meat is tender. Meanwhile, clean and cut the vegetables into small cubes. When the meat is cooked, remove it from the pan and cut it into small cubes. Mix with vegetables, return to the water and cook until carrots are tender. Add seasoning and serve.

Nutritional values per 1 cup:

Carbohydrates 3g

Sugar 2.1g

Protein 22 g

Total fat 5.7g

Sodium 71 mg

Potassium 148mg

Calcium 2.2mg

Iron 4.3mg

Vitamins (vitamin A; B-6; B-12; C; D; D2; D3; K; Riboflavin; Niacin; Thiamin; K)

Calories 112

35. Lamb cutlet with hazelnut sauce

Ingredients:

1 medium lamb cutlet

½ cup of hazelnuts

1 tsp of curry

1 tbsp of olive oil

pepper to taste

Preparation:

Wash the cutlet and cook in water 15-20 minutes. Remove from pot and drain, but keep the water. Make a sauce with olive oil, curry, hazelnuts and pepper. Spread the sauce over cutlet, add some meat water and bake at 300 degrees for 15-20 minutes.

Nutritional values per 100g:

Carbohydrates 4.7g

Sugar 4.1g

Protein 29 g

Total fat 11.8g

Sodium 137 mg

Potassium 239mg

Calcium 2.9mg

Iron 2.16mg

Vitamins (vitamin A; B-6; B-12; C; D; D2; D3; K; Riboflavin; Niacin; Thiamin; K)

Calories 213

36. Grilled red pepper

Ingredients:

1 large red pepper

1 tbsp of olive oil

2 cloves of garlic

chopped parsley

Preparation:

Mix olive oil with garlic and parsley. Spread the sauce over paprika and bake in barbecue pan on low temperature for about 10-15 minutes.

Nutritional values per 100g:

Carbohydrates 6.2g

Sugar 4.4g

Protein 2g

Total fat 0.8g

Sodium 7 mg

Potassium 215mg

Calcium 2.8mg

Iron 2. 6mg

Vitamins (vitamin A; B-6; B-12; C; D; Riboflavin; Niacin; Thiamin; K)

Calories 38

37. Stewed beef and cabbage

Ingredients:

1 large beefsteak

1 cup of chopped cabbage, cooked

¼ tsp of pepper

2 tbsp of olive oil

½ cup of water

Preparation:

Cut meat into small pieces. Put in a pot and cook on a low temperature, in olive oil until tender. Add some water if necessary. When the meat tender, add cabbage and pepper. Stew on low temperature for at least 40 minutes.

Nutritional values per 100g:

Carbohydrates 8.1g

Sugar 3.2g

Protein 36.1 g

Total fat 6.9g

Sodium 157 mg

Potassium 499mg

Calcium 19.9mg

Iron 5.9mg

Vitamins (vitamin A; B-6; B-12; C; D; D2; D3; K;Thiamin; K)

Calories 234

38. Broccoli soup

Ingredients:

1 cup of broccoli

1 small carrot

1 small onion

little salt

pepper to taste

1 tbsp of coconut oil

Preparation:

Wash the onions and carrots, but do not chop them. Put them together with the broccoli in salted water and cook. When the vegetables are done, put them all together in a blender. Remaining vegetable water heat to boiling point and stir with a little oil. Cook until the mixture thickens, add the vegetables and cook for another 5-7 minutes. Serve warm.

Nutritional values for 1 cup:

Carbohydrates 15g

Sugar 5.2g

Protein 7.2 g

Total fat 4.1g

Sodium 887 mg

Potassium 376mg

Calcium 25.5mg

Iron 1.2mg

Vitamins (vitamin A;C)

Calories 120

39. Lettuce and tuna salad

Ingredients:

1 bunch of lettuce

3 cans of tuna without oil

1 tbsp of lemon juice

2 large onions

2 large tomatoes

5 olives

Preparation:

Wash and cut lettuce. Mix it with tuna. Peel and cut the onion, cut the tomato, mix with tuna and lettuce. Add lemon juice and olives.

Nutritional values for 1 cup:

Carbohydrates 19.4g

Sugar 12g

Protein 31.2g

Total fat (good monounsaturated fat) 11.5g

Sodium 141mg

Potassium 86.1mg

Calcium 43.2mg

Iron 0.31mg

Vitamins (vitamin A; B-6; B-12; C; D; D2; D3; K; Riboflavin; Niacin; Thiamin; K)

Calories 71

40. Grilled trout fillets with parsley

Ingredients:

3 thick trout fillets

1 tbsp of parsley

3 tbsp of olive oil

6 cloves of garlic

Preparation:

Mix chopped garlic with parsley and olive oil. Spread it over fish and fry in a barbecue pan for about 15-20 minutes, on both sides. Remove from the pan and use a kitchen paper to soak the excess oil.

Nutritional values per 100g:

Carbohydrates 0.2g

Sugar 0

Protein 25.2 g

Total fat 6.6g

Sodium 113.8 mg

Potassium 61mg

Calcium 29mg

Iron 0.33mg

Vitamins (vitamin A; B-6; B-12; C; D; D2; D3; K; Riboflavin; Niacin; Thiamin; K)

Calories 170

41. Cauliflower soup

Ingredients:

1 cup of cauliflower

1 small carrot

1 small onion

little pepper

1 tbsp of oil

Preparation:

Wash the onions and carrots, but do not chop them. Put them together with the cauliflower in water and cook. When the vegetables are done, put them all together in a blender. Remaining vegetable water heat to boiling point and stir with a little oil. Cook until the mixture thickens, add the vegetables and cook for another 5-7 minutes. Serve warm.

Nutritional values for 1 cup:

Carbohydrates 13g

Sugar 4.2g

Protein 6.2 g

Total fat 4.4g

Sodium 862 mg

Potassium 366mg

Calcium 24.1mg

Iron 2mg

Vitamins (vitamin A;C)

Calories 118

42. Tomato omelet

Ingredients:

3 eggs

1 large tomato

1 small onion

1 tsp of olive oil

salt to taste

Preparation:

Wash and cut tomato. Peel and cut the onion. Fry tomato and onion in olive oil for about 10-15 minutes, on a low temperature. Remove from the heat when the water evaporates. Add eggs and mix well. Fry for another 2 minutes.

Nutritional values per 100 g:

Carbohydrates 6.1g

Sugar 2g

Protein 20g

Total fat (good monounsaturated fat) 12g

Sodium 176mg

Potassium 173mg

Calcium 15.9mg

Iron 1.9mg

Vitamins (vitamin A; B-6; B-12; C)

Calories 184

43. Grilled salmon fillet

Ingredients:

1 large salmon fillet

1 tbsp of lemon juice

2 tbsp of olive oil

1 tbsp of ground chili pepper

Preparation:

Wash the fillet and pat dry using a kitchen paper. Sprinkle some lemon juice on it and fry in a small barbecue pan for about 15-20 minutes, on a very high temperature. Remove from the pan and soak the excess oil with a kitchen paper. Add ground chili pepper before serving.

Nutritional values per 100 g:

Carbohydrates 2.9

Sugar 0.8g

Protein 24g

Total fat (good monounsaturated fat) 14.6g

Sodium 63mg

Potassium 374mg

Calcium 0.9mg

Iron 1.8mg

Vitamins (vitamin A; B-6; B-12; C)

Calories 220

44. Mixed vegetable salad:

Ingredients:

1 bunch of lettuce

1 small carrot

1 medium tomato

1 medium onion

1 small cucumber

1 medium eggplant

1 medium zucchini

1 tbsp of olive oil

1 tsp of lemon juice

Preparation:

Peel and cut eggplant and zucchini. Fry it in olive oil for 8-10 minutes. Remove from pan and soak excess oil with kitchen paper. Meanwhile, wash and cut vegetables into small pieces. Mix eggplant and zucchini with other vegetables and season with olive oil and lemon juice.

Nutritional values for one cup:

Carbohydrates 12.3g

Sugar 8.9g

Protein 11.2 g

Total fat (good monounsaturated fat) 6.5g

Sodium 176.3 mg

Potassium 95mg

Calcium 63.5mg

Iron 0.74mg

Vitamins (vitamin A; B-6; B-12; C; D; D2; D3; K; Riboflavin; Niacin; Thiamin; K)

Calories 51

45. Grilled calamari in curry sauce

Ingredients:

1 cup of frozen calamari rings

¼ cup of water

1 tsp of curry

2 tbsp of olive oil

2 cloves of garlic

1 tsp of chopped parsley

Preparation:

Make a sauce with chopped water, garlic, parsley, curry and olive oil. Fry calamari rings in a barbecue pan without oil for 7-10 minutes, on a medium temperature. You want to get a nice golden color. Add the sauce to barbecue pan with calamari and fry for few more minutes. You can add some more water if your sauce is too thick.

Nutritional values per 100g:

Carbohydrates 0.2g

Sugar 0g

Protein 19.8 g

Total fat (good monounsaturated fat) 2.8g

Sodium 96.3 mg

Potassium 0.3mg

Calcium 1.5mg

Iron 0.7mg

Vitamins (vitamin A; BD; D2; K)

Calories 92

46. Grilled sardines

Ingredients:

1 small pack (200g) of frozen sardines

4 cloves of garlic

4 tbsp of olive oil

3 tsp of tumeric

½ tsp of salt

Preparation:

Defrost and wash sardines. Make a garlic sauce with garlic, olive oil and tumeric. Spread it over sardines and fry in a barbecue pan without extra oil for about 20 minutes on a medium temperature. They should have golden-brow color before serving. Salt to taste.

Nutritional values per 100g:

Carbohydrates 0.2g

Sugar 0g

Protein 19 g

Total fat (good monounsaturated fat) 6g

Sodium 225.3 mg

Potassium 3mg

Calcium 3.5mg

Iron 3.2mg

Vitamins (vitamin A; B-6; D; D2; D3; K; Riboflavin; Niacin; Thiamin; K)

Calories 130

47. Banana shake

Ingredients:

1 large banana

2 egg whites

1.5 cup of water

1 tsp of vanilla extract

1 tbsp of agave syrup

Preparation:

Peel and chop banana into small cubes. Combine with other ingredients in a blender and mix for 30 seconds, until smooth mixture. Keep in the refrigerator and serve cold.

Nutritional values for 1 glass:

Carbohydrates 8g

Sugar 4.9g

Protein 10.2g

Total fat 2.67g

Sodium 74mg

Potassium 512.9mg

Calcium 79mg

Iron 1.88mg

Vitamins (Vitamin B-6; B-12; D; D-D2+D3)

Calories 56

48. Grilled green peppers

Ingredients:

2 green peppers

1 tbsp of olive oil

2 cloves of garlic

chopped parsley

Preparation:

Mix the olive oil with garlic and parsley.
Spread the sauce over peppers and fry in a
barbecue pan on a low temperature for about
10-15 minutes. Stir constantly.

Nutritional values per 100g:

Carbohydrates 5g

Sugar 2.2g

Protein 1.8 g

Total fat 0.4g

Sodium 4.3 mg

Potassium 191mg

Calcium 2.5mg

Iron 1.8mg

Vitamins (vitamin A; B-6; B-12; C; D; D2; D3; K; Riboflavin; Niacin; Thiamin; K)

Calories 27

49. Seafood salad

Ingredients:

1 small pack (200g) of frozen mixed seafood

3 tbsp of olive oil

1 medium onion

¼ tsp of salt

¼ cup of water (optional)

Preparation

Fry frozen seafood without oil until tender (try the octopus, it takes the most time to tender). You can add some water if necessary. Remove from frying pan and allow it to cool for about an hour. Peel and finely chop the onion. Mix it with seafood and add olive oil. This salad is best cold. Let it stand in the refrigerator for few hours before serving.

Nutritional values per 1 cup:

Carbohydrates 3.45g

Sugar 1.68g

Protein 25.8 g

Total fat 16.4g

Sodium 827mg

Potassium 453mg

Calcium 13.5mg

Iron 10mg

Vitamins (Vitamin C; B-6; B-12; A-RAE; A-IU;
E; D; D-D2+D3; K; Thianin; Riboflavin; Niacin)

Calories 280

50. Grilled zucchini with garlic

Ingredients:

1 large zucchini

4 cloves of garlic

1 tbsp of olive oil

¼ tsp of salt

Preparation:

Peel and cut zucchini into thick slices. Chop garlic and fry it for few minutes in olive oil, until nice gold color. Add zucchini and fry for another 10 minutes on a low temperature. Sprinkle with some chopped parsley before serving. Salt to taste.

Nutritional values for 1 slice:

Carbohydrates 3.6g

Sugar 1.9g

Protein 2.9 g

Total fat 0.9g

Sodium 2.21 mg

Potassium 354mg

Calcium 0.12mg

Iron 0.2mg

Vitamins (vitamin A; B-6; B-12; C; D:K)

Calories 25

51. Baked apples

Ingredients:

2 large apples

1 tsp of cinnamon

Preparation:

Bake the apples at 300 degrees for 15 minutes. Sprinkle with cinnamon before serving.

Nutritional values per 100g:

Carbohydrates 14.8g

Sugar 10g

Protein 0.4 g

Total fat 0.3g

Sodium 1.7mg

Potassium 108mg

Calcium 0mg

Iron 0mg

Vitamins (vitamin A; C)

Calories 53

52. Grilled steak with pineapple slices

Ingredients:

1 large steak

7 pineapple slices

1 tsp of ginger

little water

pepper to taste

Preparation:

Fry pineapple slices for 5-10 minutes, slightly adding a little water. Remove pineapple slices from a frying pan and fry the steak in the same frying pan for 15-20 minutes. You can add some water while frying steak. Serve with pineapple slices and sprinkle with ginger. Pepper to taste

Nutritional values per 100g:

Carbohydrates 3.8g

Sugar 2.1g

Protein 32.9 g

Total fat 4.9g

Sodium 64 mg

Potassium 413mg

Calcium 0mg

Iron 17.8mg

Vitamins (vitamin A; B-6; B-12; C; D)

Calories 182

53. Cooked cauliflower in mint sauce

Ingredients:

1 medium cauliflower

1 tbsp of chopped mint leaves

1 tsp of ginger

1 tbsp of agave syrup

Preparation:

Clean and cut cauliflower into medium cubes. Cook it in water until tender. Remove from pot and drain well. Meanwhile, make a sauce with agave syrup, ginger and mint, by combining all the ingredients in a small bowl. Pour it over cauliflower and allow it to cool for a while before serving.

Nutritional values per 100g:

Carbohydrates 6.8g

Sugar 2.8g

Protein 1.9 g

Total fat 0.4g

Sodium 31 mg

Potassium 301mg

Calcium 2.7mg

Iron 2.3mg

Vitamins (vitamin C; K)

Calories 29

54. Mushroom soup

Ingredients:

1 cup of fresh button mushrooms

1 small carrot

1 small onion

¼ tsp of pepper

1 tbsp of oil

Preparation:

Wash the onions and carrots, but do not chop them. Put them together in a large pot, add water to cover the vegetables and cook until tender. When the vegetables are done, mix them with mushrooms and put all together in a blender. Remaining vegetable water heat to boiling point and stir with a little oil. Cook until the mixture thickens, add the vegetables and cook for another 5-7 minutes. You can decorate it with little parsley.

Nutritional values for 1 cup:

Carbohydrates 3.3g

Sugar 0.2g

Protein 1.9 g

Total fat 2.6g

Sodium 340 mg

Potassium 31mg

Calcium 0mg

Iron 0mg

Vitamins (vitamin D;K)

Calories 41

55. Trout fillet with almond and tumeric sauce

Ingredients:

1 thin slice of trout fillet

1 tsp of tumeric

1 tbsp of olive oil

½ cup of almonds

1 tsp of dried rosemary

¼ tsp of pepper

Preparation:

Wash and dry the fillet. Sprinkle with tumeric and fry in hot oil for few minutes on each side. Remove from frying pan. Make a sauce with almonds, olive oil, rosemary and pepper. Pour the sauce over the fillet and fry for another few minutes, until golden brown color.

Nutritional values per 100g:

Carbohydrates 3.7g

Sugar 0.2g

Protein 25g

Total fat 8.6g

Sodium 62 mg

Potassium 263mg

Calcium 10mg

Iron 2.5mg

Vitamins (vitamin A; B-6; B-12; C; D:K)

Calories 173

56. Trout soup

Ingredients:

1 large trout

2 small carrots

1 tbsp of olive oil

1 tsp of dried parsley

dill to taste

Preparation:

Wash and clean the fish (remove all bones).
Cook the fish in a large pot for about 20. After
the fish is done, add a little olive oil (just to
cover the bottom). Fry chopped carrots for few
minutes and add water, parsley and dill. Cook
for another 15 minutes. After about 15
minutes add the fish (whole or cut into large
chunks). Put in each plate 1 tsp of olive oil
and pour the soup.

Nutritional values per 1 cup:

Carbohydrates 3.4g

Sugar 0.9g

Protein 5.9 g

Total fat 2g

Sodium 365 mg

Potassium 123mg

Calcium 2.3mg

Iron 2.3mg

Vitamins (vitamin A; B-6; B-12; C)

Calories 46

57. Cucumber salad

Ingredients:

3 large cucumbers

6 tbsp of grated walnuts

3 tbsp of sesame seeds oil

Preparation:

Peel and cut the cucumbers into thin slices. Season with sesame seed oil and sprinkle with grated walnuts.

Nutritional values per 100g:

Carbohydrates 6.8g

Sugar 2.7g

Protein 5.9 g

Total fat 4.9g

Sodium 5.76 mg

Potassium 213mg

Calcium 5.27mg

Iron 2.1mg

Vitamins (vitamin A; B-6; B-12; C; D:K)

Calories 34

58. Grilled mushrooms with garlic sauce

Ingredients:

3 cups of fresh button mushrooms

6 cloves of garlic

3 tbsp of olive oil

¼ tsp of pepper

Preparation:

Fry mushrooms without oil in a barbecue pan on a low temperature until all the water evaporates. Meanwhile, chop garlic, add to frying pan and mix with mushrooms. Fry for few more minutes. Sprinkle with olive oil before serving. Add some pepper to taste. Serve warm.

Nutritional values for one cup:

Carbohydrates 5.2g

Sugar 1.3g

Protein 8.2 g

Total fat (good monounsaturated fat) 2.3g

Sodium 47.3 mg

Potassium 25.1mg

Calcium 13.1mg

Iron 0.61mg

Vitamins (vitamin A; B-6; B-12; C; D; D2; D3;
K; Riboflavin; Niacin; Thiamin; K)

Calories 98

59. Apple and carrot balls with cinnamon

Ingredients:

5 large apples

3 large carrots

6 tsp of cinnamon

6 tsp of agave syrup

3 tsp of lemon juice

Preparation:

Peel and grate apples and carrots. Combine with other ingredients in a blender to get a smooth mixture. Make little balls and allow them to cool them in the refrigerator for few hours.

You can add grated walnuts or almonds to this recipe. That is optional, but it will increase the proteins.

Nutritional values per 100g:

Carbohydrates 17.2g

Sugar 15.3g

Protein 9.1 g

Total fat (good monounsaturated fat) 2.3g

Sodium 147.4 mg

Potassium 625mg

Calcium 13.1mg

Iron 11.61mg

Vitamins (vitamin A; B-6; B-12; C; D; D2; D3; K; Riboflavin; Niacin; Thiamin; K)

Calories 78

60. Grilled eggplant with parsley

Ingredients:

1 small eggplant

½ cup of chopped parsley

1 tsp of olive oil

Preparation:

Peel the eggplant and cut into slices. Bake it in a barbecue pan without oil. When done, spread olive oil over it, sprinkle with parsley.

Nutritional values per slice:

Carbohydrates 7.9g

Sugar .4

Protein 7.2g

Total fat 2.21g

Sodium 53mg

Potassium 29.1mg

Calcium 13.1mg

Iron 0.38mg

Vitamins (vitamin A; B-6; B-12; C; D; D2; D3; K; Riboflavin; Niacin; Thiamin; K)

Calories 52

61.Steak salad with mushrooms

Ingredients:

1 large steak

3 cups of button mushrooms

6 tbsp of chopped parsley

1 bunch of lettuce

1 large tomato

1 large onion

1 large cucumber

4 tbsp of olive oil

Preparation:

Fry the steak without oil for 15-20 minutes. Remove from pan and cut it into medium sized pieces. Fry the mushrooms, but don't cut them. Wash and peel vegetables, mix with steak and mushrooms. Season with little olive or sesame oil.

Nutritional values for one cup:

Carbohydrates 18.6g

Sugar 11.3g

Protein 21.9g

Total fat (good monounsaturated fat) 14.2g

Sodium 153.3 mg

Potassium 89.8mg

Calcium 49.9mg

Iron 0.42mg

Vitamins (vitamin A; B-6; B-12; C; D; D2; D3; K; Riboflavin; Niacin; Thiamin; K)

Calories 79

62. Fruit shake

Ingredients:

1 cup of strawberries

1 large banana

1 slice of watermelon

½ tsp of cinnamon

½ cup of water

¼ cup of ground walnuts

Preparation:

Mix ingredients in a blender for about 30 seconds. Sprinkle with cinnamon and allow it to cool in the refrigerator for about 30 minutes. Serve with ice.

Nutritional values for 1 glass:

Carbohydrates 10.67g

Sugar 8.11g

Protein 8.65g

Total fat 2.54g

Sodium 95mg

Potassium 159.6mg

Calcium 93mg

Iron 1.03mg

Vitamins (Vitamin C total ascorbic acid; B-6; B-12; A-RAE; A-IU; E-alpha-tocopherol; D; K-phylloquinone; Thianin; Riboflavin; Niacin)

Calories 74.6

Printed in Great Britain
by Amazon

25868483R00116